Improve Your Sight-singing!

INTERMEDIATE LEVEL

Paul Harris & Mike Brewer

© 1998 by Faber Music Ltd
First published in 1998 by Faber Music Ltd
3 Queen Square London WC1N 3AU
Music and text set by Wessex Music Services
Cover design by S & M Tucker
Printed in England by Halstan & Co Ltd

ISBN 0 571 51770 6

To buy Faber Music publications or to find out about
the full range of titles available please contact your
local retailer or Faber Music sales enquiries:

Tel: +44 (0)171 833 7931
Fax: +44 (0)171 278 3817
E-mail: sales@fabermusic.co.uk
Website: http://www.fabermusic.co.uk

**FABER
MUSIC**

INTRODUCTION

Whether you are a member of a choir, a singer or instrumentalist preparing for the sight-singing tests in grade exams or simply enjoy singing with friends, the ability to sight-sing with confidence and accuracy is a most important musical skill.

Using the workbook

Improve Your Sight-singing! offers a progressive series of enjoyable and stimulating stages which, if you use them systematically, will rapidly improve your reading ability. You can either work through the book on your own at home, with a friend (perhaps a fellow member of your choir) or, if you have a teacher, during your lessons.

Each stage in the book consists of two parts: firstly, specially-written, original exercises and pieces which you should take time to prepare (pp.3-22); and secondly, unprepared tests, which offer reinforcement material and the chance to measure your rate of progress (pp.23-32).

At the top of the first page in each stage are the new features being introduced. At the end of the stage, should you want to monitor your progress, there is an assessment box.

There are four different types of exercise:

Rhythmic exercises   It is very important that you feel and maintain a steady pulse: these exercises will help develop this ability. There are at least four ways of doing them: clap or tap the lower line (the beat or pulse) while singing the upper line to 'la' (or any other syllable); tap the lower line with your foot and clap the upper line; on a table or flat surface, tap the lower line with one hand and the upper line with the other; 'play' the lower line on a metronome and clap or tap the upper line.

Melodic exercises   Once you are confident you have grasped the particular rhythmic pattern you can then focus on the melodic exercises. Fluent sight-singing is greatly improved by the ability to 'pre-hear' intervals and to recognise melodic shapes at a glance. These shapes are often related to scale and arpeggio patterns, so before you sing each exercise look through it first and see whether there are any recognisable patterns which will make your singing more fluent.

Prepared pieces   Take time to ask yourself the questions which apply to the vocal line and appear before some of the pieces, and devise more of these questions yourself. Prepare these pieces carefully as they will give you practice at many rhythmic and melodic patterns you will encounter time after time. The first exercise can be accompanied by an optional second voice singing the lower part but using the same words (perhaps your teacher or a friend) or you could play the lower line on the piano. Exercise 2 has simple (optional) piano accompaniments. Try to get a friend (or your teacher) to play them if possible – they will help you to develop the musical ideas and help you to sing in tune. You could play them yourself or, if your pianistic skills are modest, just try adding the left hand or bass line only.

Unprepared pieces   Finally, when you are confident you can sing all the work in the stage with real security, try the unprepared tests which you should read without preparation – at sight.

Some helpful suggestions have been made throughout the book but these need not be strictly adhered to. There are also references to useful tunes to help you remember intervals.

The authors wish to thank Debbie Lammin for many helpful suggestions.

Stage 1

C major in the above range

Rhythmic exercises

Don't forget to vary the syllables if you sing the top line in the rhythmic exercises. Use any syllable of your choice.

Melodic exercises

Sing the first two melodic exercises in any or all of the following ways:
- to the scale number (1, 7, 1, 3, 4, 5, 6, 4, 2, 7, 1 in exercise 1)
- to the note name (ie C, B, C, E etc.)
- to 'ma' or any syllable of your choice (remember to keep the front of your tongue down behind your lower teeth)
- to tonic sol-fa (doh, soh, me, lah, soh, ti, doh in exercise 2)

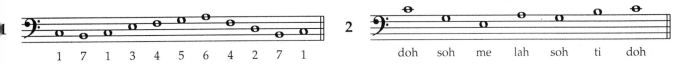

1   1   7   1   3   4   5   6   4   2   7   1   2   doh   soh   me   lah   soh   ti   doh

Now clap the following rhythm A; then clap this rhythm as you sing the exercises 1A and 2A. Don't sing these exercises too slowly (♩=144).

Hap - py, hap - py, hap - py realm, hap - py, hap - py, hap - py realm be -

- yond___ ex - press - ing, Such, such, such, such a ro - yal pair.

Words: Anon.

5 Hush ba - by, naugh - ty ba - by, Hush you squall - ing thing I say!

Prepared pieces

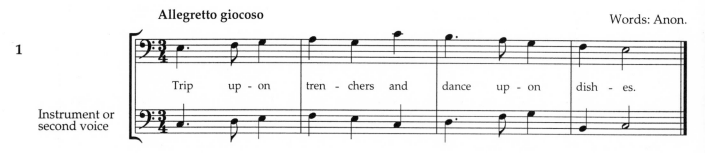

Allegretto giocoso

Words: Anon.

1

Trip up - on tren - chers and dance up - on dish - es.

Instrument or second voice

2 In which key is this song? Play the key chord and sing the arpeggio. How will you find your first note? What melodic pattern do you notice in bar 6?

Try singing the song to the syllables *na* or *ni* before you sing the words.

Moderato

mf

Words: John Byron

Some say, com - pared to Bo - non - ci - ni

5

That Fride - ric Han - del's but a nin - ny.

sfz

Self/teacher's assessment

Satisfactory	
Good	
Excellent	

Unprepared pieces: page 23

Stage 2

Rhythmic exercises

Melodic exercises

Don't forget to sing the melodic exercises to scale numbers, note names or any syllable of your choice. Then try them to *la*.

Allegro

mf

Antonin Dvořák

Though you have a lit - tle home and fire - side I shall ne - ver be your lov - ing bride, I shall ne - ver, I shall ne - ver in your strong arms lie.

Words: Jonathan Swift

Daph - ne knows, with e - qual ease how to vex and how to please.

Prepared pieces

1 Try singing the following exercise slowly to *ning* before singing the actual words.

2 In which key is this song? Play the key chord and sing the arpeggio. The notes of bars 3 and 4 all belong to a melodic pattern. What is the pattern called? How will you achieve the appropriate character in your performance?

To add clarity to the diction place the final consonant at the very beginning of the rest that follows, e.g.

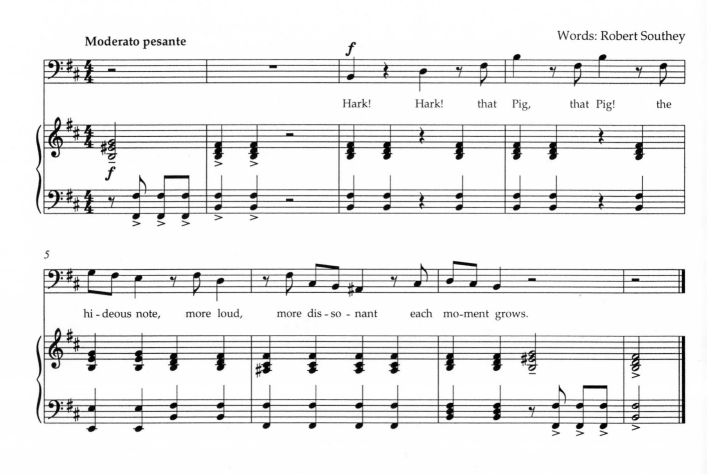

Self/teacher's assessment

Satisfactory	
Good	
Excellent	

Unprepared pieces: page 24

Stage 3

Octaves ♪♪

Rhythmic exercises

Whisper the following exercises to *puh*. Can you feel your breathing muscles working?

Melodic exercises

Sing the next two exercises to any syllables of your choice.

Try the next three exercises imitating a trumpet-like sound; use the syllables *ba* or *pa* or make up one yourself.

Words: C.S. Caverley

On, on the ves-sel steals; Round go the pad-dle wheels And now the tou-rist feels, As he should.

Prepared pieces

Words: Lewis Carroll

1

Instrument or
second voice

How doth the lit - tle cro - co - dile Im - prove his shin - ing tale?

2 This song has three phrases. Compare the rhythm of each phrase. How
will the piano introduction help you to find the first four notes? What
character will you give the song?

Allegro giocoso *mf* Words: Anon.

My name is George Na-tha-niel Cur-zon I am a most su-pe-rior per-son

5

My face is pink, my hair is sleek I dine at Blen-heim once a week.

Self/teacher's assessment

Satisfactory	
Good	
Excellent	

Useful tunes:
The following tunes begin with an octave:
Ascending: Somewhere over the rainbow
Descending: The minstrel boy

Unprepared pieces: page 25

Stage 4

$\frac{3}{8}$

Rhythmic exercises

You might like to sing this set of exercises to the syllable *bah*.

Melodic exercises

Clap this rhythm ♩♪ ♩♪ ♫ as you sing the next exercises.

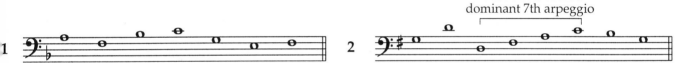

These notes form a dominant 7th arpeggio

Can you identify a sequence in the next exercise?

What melodic patterns can you spot in the next two exercises?

Words: W.M. Praed

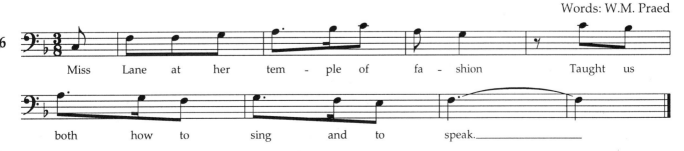

Miss Lane at her tem – ple of fa – shion Taught us

both how to sing and to speak.

Prepared pieces

1 How do the two phrases in the next piece differ?

Words: Edward Lear

Instrument or second voice

How plea - sant to know Mis - ter Lear

4

Who has writ - ten such vo - lumes of stuff! _____

2 In which key is this song? Play the key chord and hum the arpeggio. What pattern is formed by the first three notes you will sing? How will you find your first note? Remember to give clarity to the final consonants.

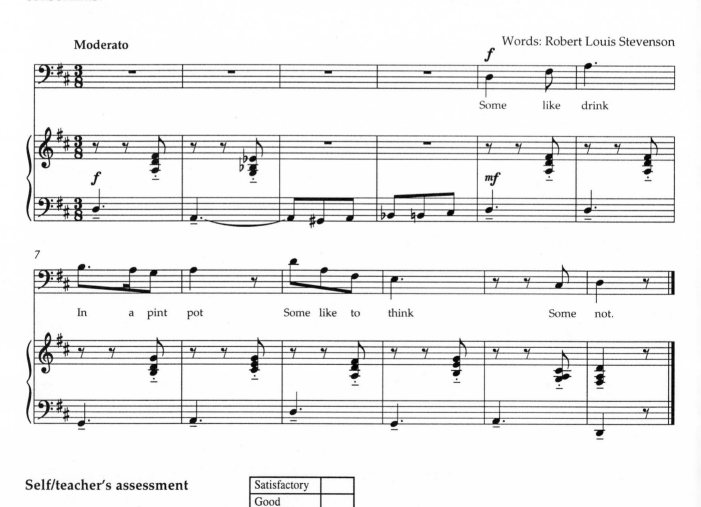

Words: Robert Louis Stevenson

Moderato

Some like drink

7

In a pint pot Some like to think Some not.

Self/teacher's assessment

Satisfactory	
Good	
Excellent	

Unprepared pieces: page 26

Stage 5

$\frac{6}{8}$

Rhythmic exercises

Try improvising a simple melody to each of the following rhythmic exercises.

Melodic exercises

Try any syllable of your choice or the syllable *ya*.

Words: Anon.

She tells me with cla - ret she can - not a - gree And she thinks of a hogs-head when-e'er she sees me.

12

Prepared pieces

Words: Anon.

1

Rub - a - dub - dub Three men in a tub, And how do you think they got there?

Instrument or
second voice

2 In which key is this song? Play the key note and sing the arpeggio.
What is the purpose of the B♮ in bar 5? How many bars are based on
scale or arpeggio patterns?

Moderato con moto

Words: Harry Graham

mp

Bil - ly in one of his nice new sash-es

mp *sempre legato*

5

Fell in the fire and was burnt to ash - es; Now, al - though the room grows chil - ly, I

9

poco rit.

have - n't the heart to poke poor Bil - ly.

Self/teacher's assessment

Satisfactory	
Good	
Excellent	

Unprepared pieces: page 27

Stage 6

Rhythmic exercises

You may like to sing the top line using the syllables *la* or *ma* to produce a very smooth legato in the next set of rhythmic exercises. Then try *da*, gently flicking the top of your tongue for each 'D'.

Melodic exercises

Sing the next two exercises very smoothly.

In contrast sing the next exercise *staccato* using the syllable *ka*. Be aware of the movements of the back of your tongue as you make each articulation.

Words: Thomas Love Peacock

The rich man has a kit - chen And cooks to dress his din - ner.

Prepared pieces

Words: Alexander Lyell

1

Oh lit-tle Ma-ry___ I don't see Why you don't fol-low me down to the sea.

Instrument or
second voice

2 How will you find your first note? How do the two phrases in the song
differ? In which key is the song? Play the key chord and sing the
arpeggio.

Practise producing a short aspirate 'h' clearly but gently. You might
like to sing the song to *ha*, then identify the words that begin with 'h'
before singing the song as printed.

Allegretto

Words: Samuel Johnson

mf

mf leggiero

I put my hat up - on my head And walked in - to the Strand,

6

And there I met a - no - ther man Whose hat was in his___ hand.

Self/teacher's assessment

Satisfactory	
Good	
Excellent	

Unprepared pieces: page 28

Stage 7

6ths

Rhythmic exercises

Try singing the syllable *wa* when you sing the following rhythmic exercises; add it to your ever-growing list of syllables.

Melodic exercises

In the next exercises try double consonants, e.g. *dwa*, *nya* or *gla*. Make up more of your own.

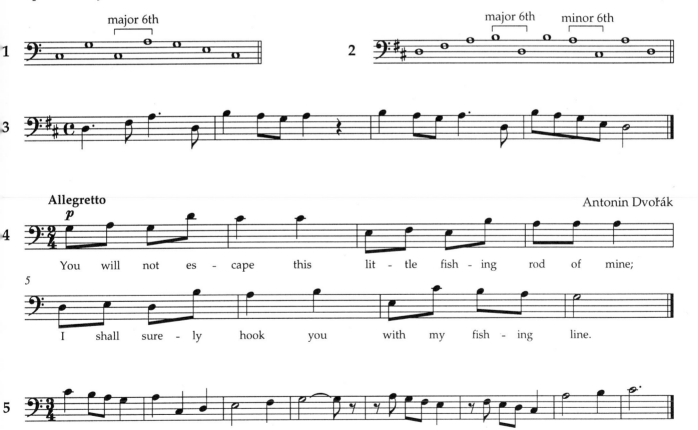

Allegretto

p

Antonin Dvořák

4 You will not es - cape this lit - tle fish - ing rod of mine;

5 I shall sure - ly hook you with my fish - ing line.

Words: William Shakespeare

6 Friends, Ro - mans and coun - try - men, lend me your ears.

Prepared pieces

Words: Thomas Gray

1

From hence, ye beau-ties, un-de-ceived, Know one false step is ne'er re-trieved.

Instrument or second voice

2 In which key is this piece? Play the key chord and sing the arpeggio. The intervals of a fifth and a sixth both occur in the vocal line of the song; can you find them? How will you find your first note?

Words: Bret Harte

Andante — *p espress.*

Do I sleep? Do I dream? Do I won - der and doubt? Are

5

things what they seem? Or are vi - sions a - bout?

rit.

dim.

Self/teacher's assessment

Satisfactory	
Good	
Excellent	

Useful tunes:
The following tunes begin with a major 6th:
Ascending: My bonny lies over the ocean
                   The holly and the ivy
Descending: Salut d'amour (Edward Elgar)
                   Nobody knows

Unprepared pieces: page 29

Stage 8

 E minor

Rhythmic exercises

You might try singing the upper line in the next exercises to *Du, du-be-du-be du* or *Da, da-va-da-va da* — alternatively, make up your own syllables.

Melodic exercises

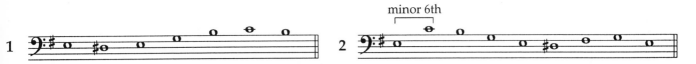

You could try using *so, su* or *si* in the next exercises. How will this help you in exercise 6?

Words: John Gay

My pas - sion— is as mus - tard— strong; I sit, all so - ber— sad.

Prepared pieces

Words: Anon.

1

Instrument or
second voice

Have you not— in a chim-ney seen A sul-len pine-log, wet— and— green?

2 In which key is this piece? Play the key chord and sing the arpeggio.
The first four notes in bar 3 are based on which pattern? Can you spot
a pattern in bar 4?

Moderato   *mf*   Words: Anon.

Three— child-ren slid-ing on the ice   Up-

mf

3

-on a sum-mers day   As— it fell out, they all fell in, The rest they ran a - way.

Self/teacher's assessment

Satisfactory	
Good	
Excellent	

Useful tunes:
The following tunes begin with a minor 6th:
Ascending: 'Close every door' from *Joseph and his amazing*
technicoloured dream coat
Descending: All things bright and beautiful

Unprepared pieces: page 30

Stage 9

Rhythmic exercises

Melodic exercises

Notice how the rhythmic patterns are repeated in the following four
exercises. Use short, light syllables.

Sing the next exercise quite slowly. Try to identify the 'm's
(humming consonants).

Words: A.D. Godfrey

Prepared pieces

1

Words: J.K. Stephens

Birth-days? yes in a ge-ne-ral way; for the most if not for the best of men.

Instrument or second voice

2 How will you give character to this song? In which key is the song?
Play the key chord and sing the arpeggio. Clap the rhythm.

Allegretto

Words: Godfrey Turner

That's ra - ther a queer sort of sto - ry I hear, Set a -

- bout to ex - plain Why Sir John went to Spain, And his

fa - mi-ly too with, of course lit-tle Lou. Yes it pos-sib-ly may have been just as you say.

Self/teacher's assessment

Satisfactory	
Good	
Excellent	

Unprepared pieces: page 31

Stage 10

Rhythmic exercises

Melodic exercises

To improve your legato singing you may like to try the syllable
oo in the following exercises. Feel the tingle in your top lip!

Words: William Shakespeare

Is this a dag - ger I see be - fore me the han - dle to - ward my hand?

Prepared pieces

1

Words: Jonathan Swift

Soothed with the time___ the King grew vain, Fought all___ his bat — tles o'er a-gain.

Instrument or second voice

2 What does *Molto giocoso* mean? How will you interpret this in your performance? How will you find your first note? In which key is the song? Play the key chord and sing the arpeggio.

Words: J.K. Stephens

Molto giocoso

There are___ peo-ple, I know to be found, who

say, and ap — pa — rent — ly think That so — rrow and care may be

drowned___ by a time — ly con — sump — tion of drink.___

Self/teacher's assessment

Satisfactory	
Good	
Excellent	

Unprepared pieces: page 32

Unprepared Pieces - Stage 1

Thomas F. Walmisley

Music, all pow'r - ful o'er the hu - man mind! Can still each men - tal storm, each tu - mult calm;

Hungarian Trad.

Allegretto

Chi - ffa, chi - ffa cha - ffa, go - ing by train, Chi - tter, chi - tter cha - tter, rush - ing through rain; Through the green fields, ov - er wide plain; Chi - ffa, chi - ffa cha - ffa, go - ing by train.

Stage 2

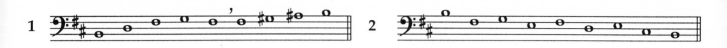

Anton Bruckner (adapted)

Li - be - ra me, Do - mi - ne, de mor - te ae - ter - na,

in di - e il - la, il - la tre - men - da;

Gabriel Fauré

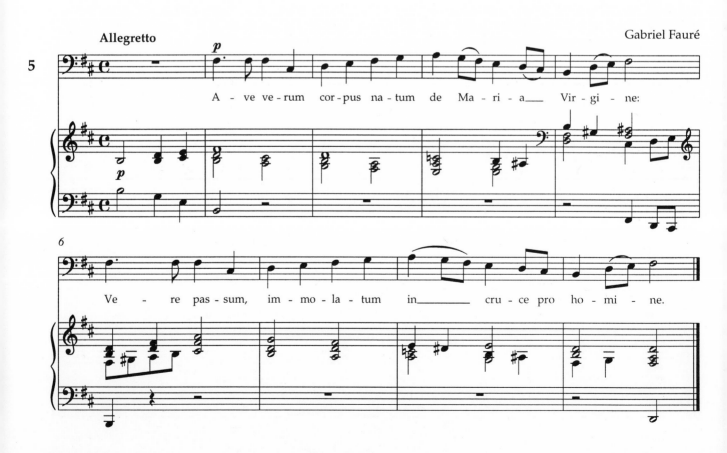

A - ve ve - rum cor - pus na - tum de Ma - ri - a___ Vir - gi - ne:

Ve - re pas - sum, im - mo - la - tum in___ cru - ce pro ho - mi - ne.

Stage 3

Moderato

Henry Purcell

So we, that are thy peo - ple and the sheep of___ thy___ pas - ture, shall give thee thanks for e - - ver.

Langsam (Slow)

Robert Schumann

Un - der the crim - son flo - wers slum - ber now, slum - ber now, Oh ti - ny bird! Un - der the crim - son flo - wers there you lie mute, your song un - heard, un - der the crim - son flo - wers slum - ber now, slum - ber now oh ti - ny bird!

Stage 4

Johannes Brahms

When ro - ses flou - rish in blos - - som, then love_____ will cast_____ its lit - - tle net.

Andantino quasi allegretto

Antonin Dvořák

By an an - cient foun - - tain stands a fair young mai - - den "Tell me, oh tell me my dear - est, Oh, dar - ling, do you tru - ly love me?"

Stage 5

Moderato

Johann Walter

O Je - su par - vu - le_____ I long for thee___ al - way___

Hear me, I be - seech thee___ O pu - er op - ti - me.___

Andante

Charles Villiers Stanford

mf

Oh the high val - ley the lit - tle low hill and the corn field ov - er the sea,

rit.

Oh the grey is - land the haze the hea - ther and scent of the gorse in the air.

Stage 6

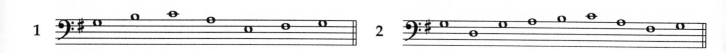

1  2

3

Felix Mendelssohn

4

Na - tions, give thanks to the Lord. Wor - ship the Lord with glad - ness.

How can you contrast the two halves of the next piece?

Allegro moderato

Trad.

5

Oh no it is not a__ no - ble, no-ble knight Nor_ a - ny_ gen - tle_

man But_ I have been wooed by_ young_ Wil - liam Who is one_ of your ser - ving men.

Stage 7

Allegretto

Antonin Dvořák

You will not es - cape this lit - tle fish - ing rod of mine;

I shall sure - ly hook you with my fish - ing line.

How will you find your first note in the next piece?

Johannes Brahms

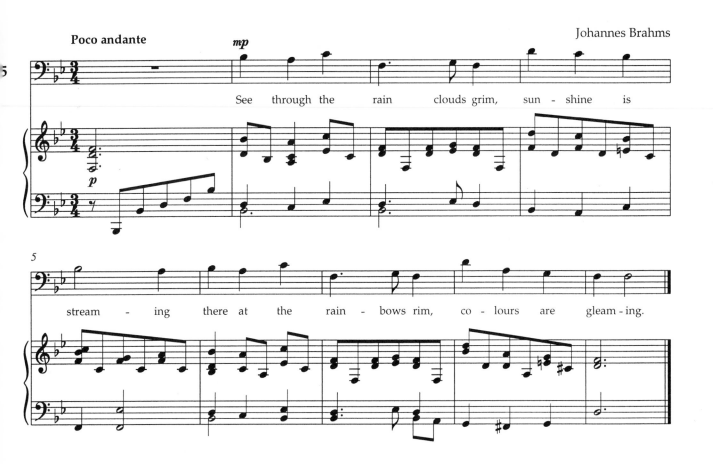

See through the rain clouds grim, sun - shine is

stream - ing there at the rain - bows rim, co - lours are gleam - ing.

Stage 8

Pyotr Ilyich Tchaikovsky

Lento

See___ now___ the___ sa - cri - fice___ raised on high___ for

us, raised on___ high_____ for us.

Allegro moderato

Edward German

It was a lo - ver and his lass, with a

hey,_____ and a ho,_____ with a hey, and a ho, and a

hey___ no - ni - no, hey_____ no - ni - no.

Stage 10

1 **2**

3

Allegro giusto

Franz Schubert

4

The young live— for— plea-sure in talk and in dreams, ca-rous-ing— and— romp-ing and

dan - cing, but sighs and— com - plain-ings will tell, so— it— seems, that

mo - ment when age is ad - van - - - - cing.

Moderato

Trad.

5

Lord Lov-ell was bu-ried in the low-er chan-cel the o-ther was bu-ried in the

high'r_____ In a year or two or three at the most I'll re-turn to my La-dy Nan-cy.